Faith in Mirrors

Faith in Mirrors

Reflections That Tell a Story

HOUSTON HEFLIN

RESOURCE *Publications* • Eugene, Oregon

FAITH IN MIRRORS
Reflections That Tell a Story

Copyright © 2024 Houston Heflin. All rights reserved. Except for brief quotations in critical publications or reviews, no part of this book may be reproduced in any manner without prior written permission from the publisher. Write: Permissions, Wipf and Stock Publishers, 199 W. 8th Ave., Suite 3, Eugene, OR 97401.

Resource Publications
An Imprint of Wipf and Stock Publishers
199 W. 8th Ave., Suite 3
Eugene, OR 97401

www.wipfandstock.com

PAPERBACK ISBN: 979-8-3852-2549-1
HARDCOVER ISBN: 979-8-3852-2550-7
EBOOK ISBN: 979-8-3852-2551-4

VERSION NUMBER 080824

To everyone
who receives
riddles and mysteries
as gifts from a playful God.

Contents

Introduction | ix

Great Offering | 2
Good Samaritan | 4
Wise Building | 6
Humble Prayer | 8
God's Image | 10
Losing Jesus | 12
Seventy Sevens | 14
Two Prodigals | 16
Persistent Widow | 18
Ten Men | 20
Bartimaeus Sees | 22
Suffering Woman | 24
Jairus' Daughter | 26
Seeking Saving | 28
Disciples Protest | 30
Living Water | 32
True Obedience | 34
Water Walking | 36
Listening Worrying | 38
One Sheep | 40
One Coin | 42
Thomas Faith | 44

Mustard Seed | 46
Hidden Treasure | 48
Angels Fish | 50
Healing Faith | 52
Disciples Defect | 54
Entering Jerusalem | 56
Jesus Baptized | 58
Nathaniel Believes | 60
Loving Family | 62
Baby Gifts | 64
Refugee Family | 66
Jesus' Birth | 68
Wedding Wine | 70
Pilate's Questions | 72
John's Identity | 74
Washing Feet | 76
Roof Access | 78
Calling Levi | 80
Jesus Tested | 82
Stubborn Hearts | 84
Rejected Prophet | 86
Resurrection News | 88
Jesus' Family | 90
Centurion Faith | 92
Save Yourself | 94
Feeding Thousands | 96
Killing Lazarus | 98
Teaching Authority | 100
Last Workers | 102

Index of Scriptures | 105

Introduction

Each of these mirror poems was created to be read both forwards and backwards, offering fresh encounters with familiar moments in Jesus' life. The forward reading is on the left and the backwards reading is on the right. As you read the poems backwards, you'll see how the reflection tells a different side of the story, either from another person or another point of view. Part of the joy these poems bring is interpreting who the two voices might be.

A close cousin to mirror poems is the palindrome, where the same message is communicated forwards and backwards with letters. These mirror poems here differ from palindromes in two important ways: first, they read forwards and backwards by word or phrase, not by individual letters. Second, the backwards reading reveals a new meaning or perspective.

For example, Jesus welcomed children and said to his disciples,

> "Let them come.
> Do not
> stop them."

The backwards reading presents the attitude and perspective of the disciples who turned away parents who were bringing children to Jesus:

> "Stop them.
> Do not
> let them come."

Introduction

As another example, after the parable of the vineyard workers who were hired throughout the day, Jesus says these words:

> "The first
> will be
> the last."

He then completes the mirror poem by stating the opposite:

> "The last
> will be
> the first."

The mirror poems in this collection expand on this pattern, introducing new insights into familiar stories. Each poem functions like a mirror where faith often appears in the reflection.

Writing these poems nudged me into the Bible to pay attention, watching for details I often overlook, experiencing Jesus in new ways. I hope reading these poems will do the same for you.

Great Offering

Mark 12:41–44

> A wealthy person
> gives more at the offering than
> a poor widow.
> "I am giving everything
> out of my wealth.
> I am not giving
> all I have."

"All I have.
I am not giving
out of my wealth.
I am giving everything."
A poor widow
gives more at the offering than
a wealthy person.

Good Samaritan

Luke 10:25–37

> Heartless!
> I was not
> at the right place, at the right time.
> I was just
> a man attacked, beaten, and left for dead
> as a priest and a Levite walked by.
> I couldn't believe it,
> a Samaritan stops to bandage wounds.
> Not many people would guess that
> a donkey would become a stretcher
> and
> a hotel would become a hospital
> until he comes around again.
> I know who my neighbor is.

I know who my neighbor is.
Until he comes around again,
a hotel would become a hospital
and
a donkey would become a stretcher.
Not many people would guess that
a Samaritan stops to bandage wounds.
I couldn't believe it,
as a priest and a Levite walked by;
a man attacked, beaten, and left for dead.
I was just
at the right place, at the right time.
I was not
heartless.

Wise Building

Matthew 7:24–27

Where will you build your life's house?
The sunny days offer a choice,
the stormy days deliver a test.
I chose wisely, building on rock.
When the storms come
others will say,
"I am the foolish person."
You never want to be saying,
"I wish I had chosen another foundation."
Choosing sand has consequences.
When the rains come down
it will fall with a great crash!

It will fall with a great crash
when the rains come down!
Choosing sand has consequences.
I wish I had chosen another foundation.
You never want to be saying,
"I am the foolish person."
Others will say
when the storms come,
"I chose wisely, building on rock."
The stormy days deliver a test,
the sunny days offer a choice.
Where will you build your life's house?

Humble Prayer

Luke 18:9–14

> The arrogant Pharisee
> prayed differently than
> the humble sinner:
> "God, I thank you!
> All I can say is,
> I am not like other people,
> thieves and tax collectors.
> I am just like
> what you want me to be.
> I am so far away from
> anything else.
> I have no need to say
> 'God have mercy on me, a sinner.'"

"God have mercy on me, a sinner.
I have no need to say
anything else.
I am so far away from
what you want me to be.
I am just like
thieves and tax collectors.
I am not like other people.
All I can say is,
'God, I thank you.'
The humble sinner
prayed differently than
the arrogant Pharisee.

God's Image

Mark 12:13–17

> "Give to Caesar what is Caesar's
> and
> return what belongs to me.
> My image is imprinted there
> on your coins
> not
> on your hearts
> where value truly lies.
> You will find my image
> everywhere in my kingdom."

"Everywhere in my Kingdom
you will find my image,
where value truly lies:
on your hearts,
not
on your coins.
My image is imprinted there.
Return what belongs to me,
and
give to Caesar what is Caesar's."

Losing Jesus

Luke 2:41–50

Outside Jerusalem
terror strikes a mom's heart;
losing her child,
desperate to hold him again.
Searching and
finding no consolation,
only weeping in Jerusalem.
For three days
overcome and reacting with fear,
furious, disappointed, and angry.
The teachers of the law
were astonished at his words;
also, his parents.
Obeying,
teaching,
listening,
"I had to be
in my Father's house,
doing my Father's work."
He would be lost three days
a second time in his life.

A second time in his life
he would be lost three days.
"Doing my Father's work
in my Father's house,
I had to be
listening,
teaching,
obeying."
Also, his parents
were astonished at his words.
The teachers of the law:
furious, disappointed, and angry,
overcome and reacting with fear.
For three days
only weeping in Jerusalem,
finding no consolation.
Searching and
desperate to hold him again,
losing her child,
terror strikes a mom's heart
outside Jerusalem.

Seventy Sevens

Matthew 18:21–22

>When a sibling has sinned against you
>forgiveness must be offered.
>How many times
>you should forgive?
>One might guess,
>it is more than
>seven, yes?

Seven? Yes!
It is more than
one might guess
you should forgive.
How many times?
Forgiveness must be offered
when a sibling has sinned against you.

Two Prodigals

Luke 15:11–32

                    Love
                      of
                  riches!
        From a father's wealth,
          the prodigal at home;
                he sought
              a lavish party.
    Wasting treasure to celebrate,
                    then
    losing it all in a distant land.
            That loss hit hard.
          Life was so much better
            when he was at home.
    If only he were in his father's house.
                    Yes,
            on a father's mercy
                    rely,
                    and
                come home!

Come home
and
rely
on a father's mercy!
Yes!
If only he were in his father's house.
When he was at home
life was so much better.
That loss hit hard.
Losing it all in a distant land,
then …
wasting treasure to celebrate!
A lavish party!
He sought the prodigal;
at home!
From a father's wealth:
riches
of
love!

Persistent Widow

Luke 18:1–8

>In our town
>justice needs to be done.
>I know what I have to do.
>It's bothering me,
>a widow, pleading,
>"Grant me justice against my adversary!"
>I'm tired of hearing
>"No!"
>I don't care what people think,
>I will persist.

I will persist.
I don't care what people think.
"No!"
I'm tired of hearing,
"Grant me justice against my adversary!"
A widow pleading,
it's bothering me.
I know what I have to do:
justice needs to be done
in our town.

Ten Men

Luke 17:11–19

> I believe gratitude is important.
> I should go back and say thank you.
> Did no one else think this?
> Jesus said,
> "Where are the others?
> Your faith has made you well."

"Your faith has made you well.
Where are the others?"
Jesus said,
"Did no one else think this:
'I should go back and say thank you'?
I believe gratitude is important."

Bartimaeus Sees

Mark 10:46–52

> Have faith!
> The wounded can choose to
> take a chance and ask.
> I decided to
> call for him.
> Jesus said,
> "What do you want?"
> Does a blind man know what he wants?
> I want to see!

I want to see:
does a blind man know what he wants?
"What do you want?"
Jesus said,
"Call for him."
I decided to
take a chance and ask.
The wounded can choose to
have faith.

Suffering Woman

Mark 5:24–34

> Her 12 years of suffering ended
> when
> she acted with faith.
> Jesus was touched,
> and then both had a sense,
> feeling transferring power,
> the healer and the healed.
> Who was touching him
> (not appearing to know
> the crowd was
> touching his garment)?
> She fell at his feet and said, "I was."
> Kneeling down,
> he said,
> "Your faith has healed you."

"Your faith has healed you,"
he said.
Kneeling down,
she fell at his feet and said, "I was
touching his garment."
The crowd was
not appearing to know
who was touching him.
The healer and the healed,
feeling transferring power.
And then both had a sense
Jesus was touched
she acted with faith
when
her 12 years of suffering ended.

Jairus' Daughter

Mark 5:35–43

Believe!
Jesus said,
while
outside the room.
The mourners cried,
"She is dead.
How can you say
'She is only sleeping?'"
The mourners were
laughing.
Jesus was not.
And
"Little girl, get up!"
he commanded her.

He commanded her,
"Little girl, get up!"
and
Jesus was not
laughing.
The mourners were.
"She is only sleeping.
How can you say,
'She is dead?'"
The mourners cried
outside the room
while
Jesus said,
believe!

Seeking Saving

Luke 19:1–10

>Out of the tall crowds,
>climbing a Sycamore tree,
>a wealthy tax collector
>seeks
>Jesus.
>"Come down,
>I'm coming to your house today."
>He gave his possessions
>to those in need.
>Jesus came to seek and save the lost.

Jesus came to seek and save the lost.
To those in need,
he gave his possessions.
"I'm coming to your house today,
come down."
Jesus
seeks
a wealthy tax collector
climbing a Sycamore tree,
out of the tall crowds.

Disciples Protest

Matthew 19:13–15

> The Kingdom belongs
> to those like children,
> yet
> the disciples protested
> as
> children approached Jesus
> to receive a blessing.
> "Let them come!
> Do not
> stop them."

"Stop them.
Do not
let them come
to receive a blessing."
Children approached Jesus
as
the disciples protested.
Yet
to those like children
the Kingdom belongs.

Living Water

John 4:1–26

> "Give me this water to drink,"
> a stranger at the well
> asks,
> and
> she is no longer alone.
> How different they are:
> gender, and class,
> but
> how similar they are:
> mistreated and rejected.
> She needed no husband,
> and she embraced the questions,
> "Where can you get living water?"
> "Are you greater than Jacob?"
> "Where should we worship?"
> Good questions.
> Discussing
> a prophet,
> and
> the awaited Messiah?
> "I am he."

"I am he."
The awaited Messiah,
and
a prophet,
discussing
good questions.
"Where should we worship?"
"Are you greater than Jacob?"
"Where can you get living water?"
And she embraced the questions.
She needed no husband.
Mistreated and rejected,
how similar they are.
But
gender, and class,
how different they are.
She is no longer alone,
and
asks
a stranger at the well,
"Give me this water to drink!"

True Obedience

Matthew 21:28–31

> Only one son obeyed.
> Neither did what they said:
> one promised action,
> one promised inaction.
> "When Dad said go work in the field
> I decided I would go,
> but
> I didn't do what I said I would do."

"I didn't do what I said I would do
but
I decided I would go,
when Dad said go work in the field."
One promised inaction,
one promised action.
Neither did what they said.
Only one son obeyed.

Water Walking

Matthew 14:22–33

             Strolling on the lake before dawn,
                        Jesus appeared,
                              that day
                                Peter
                      will never forget.
                        The disciples
                              in awe!
                   A person on the water
                   walking toward them.
                        The figure said,
                              "Come."
              As Peter stepped out of the boat
              the waves were between them
                  but fear swelled as well.
          Two people were walking on water
                        for a moment.
                   Humiliated and sinking
                      Peter found himself
                           soaking wet
                   climbing into the boat.
                          Jesus said,
                     "Why did you doubt?"

"Why did you doubt?"
Jesus said,
climbing into the boat.
Soaking wet,
Peter found himself
humiliated and sinking
for a moment.
Two people were walking on water!
But fear swelled as well.
The waves were between them
as Peter stepped out of the boat.
"Come."
the figure said,
walking toward them;
a person on the water.
In awe,
the disciples
will never forget
Peter
that day
Jesus appeared
strolling on the lake before dawn.

Listening Worrying

Luke 10:38–42

>When Jesus is in your home
>you have two choices.
>Some might say,
>"The preparations must be made!"
>This was Martha's cry,
>"My sister won't help me!"
>"You are worried about many things;
>only one thing is needed"
>Jesus said.
>Listening at Jesus' feet,
>Mary chose what is better.

Mary chose what is better:
Listening at Jesus' feet.
Jesus said,
"Only one thing is needed.
You are worried about many things."
"My sister won't help me!"
This was Martha's cry:
"The preparations must be made!"
Some might say
you have two choices
when Jesus is in your home.

One Sheep

Luke 15:3–7

> It is essential to ask,
> "How many sheep
> must wander away
> before the good shepherd
> must wander away?"
> You'll find, only one.

You'll find only one
must wander away
before the good shepherd
must wander away.
"How many sheep?"
It is essential to ask.

One Coin

Luke 15:8–10

A woman's lost coin
means more than
it
appears.
It
is life;
something incomparable in this parable,
something devastating to lose.
To find it,
light a lamp,
sweep the house,
search carefully.
When one is found,
the angels rejoice in heaven.

The angels rejoice in heaven
when one is found.
Search carefully,
sweep the house,
light a lamp
to find it;
something devastating to lose.
Something incomparable in this parable,
is life.
It
appears
it
means more than
a woman's lost coin.

Thomas Faith

John 20:24–29

> Although once doubting,
> after touching and seeing;
> now having faith
> in him.
> I want him to know I believe!

I want him to know I believe
in him,
now having faith;
after touching and seeing,
although once doubting.

Mustard Seed

Mark 4:30–32

The Kingdom of God
transforms
each person
with faith,
like the smallest mustard seed planted
just needs the right soil
to grow
the largest garden plant,
hosting birds in its branches.

Hosting birds in its branches,
the largest garden plant,
to grow,
just needs the right soil.
Like the smallest mustard seed planted
with faith,
each person
transforms
the Kingdom of God.

Hidden Treasure

Matthew 13:44

>Great joy!
He found
riches.
Selling all
to buy the field.
Buried and discovered,
concealed and uncovered;
twice hidden treasure
is
the Kingdom of God
for the one who seeks.

For the one who seeks,
the Kingdom of God
is
twice hidden treasure:
concealed and uncovered,
buried and discovered.
To buy the field,
selling all
riches.
He found
great joy!

Angels Fish

Matthew 13:47–50

> Those who fish
> saving
> time
> at the end of
> the day,
> while waiting for
> good and bad
> separating,
> like
> angels.

Angels
like
separating
good and bad,
while waiting for
the day
at the end of
time,
saving
those who fish.

Healing Faith

Luke 5:12–14

> I want to be healed.
> It will be done
> if you say,
> "I am willing."

I am willing
if you say,
"It will be done.
I want to be healed."

Disciples Defect

John 6:60–69

> At hearing hard teachings,
> when others are turning away,
> you do not want to leave, too?
> These are words of eternal life.
> The Holy One of God is speaking.

The Holy One of God is speaking.
These are words of eternal life.
You do not want to leave, too,
when others are turning away
at hearing hard teachings.

Entering Jerusalem

Matthew 21:1–11

Hosanna, yes!
The crowds shouted,
"Blessed
is he
who comes
in the name of the Lord!"
With palm branches spread,
here he comes, riding on a donkey.

Here he comes riding on a donkey,
with palm branches spread.
"In the name of the Lord,
who comes?
Is he
blessed?"
The crowds shouted,
Hosanna, yes!

Jesus Baptized

Matthew 3:13–17

God said, "I love my son,"
and
the Spirit-dove descended
at the Jordan river.
"It is right to do this."
Jesus said,
"I need to be baptized by you."
John protested
before consenting.

Before consenting,
John protested,
"I need to be baptized by *you!*"
Jesus said,
"It is right to do this
at the Jordan river."
The Spirit-dove descended,
and
God said, "I love my son."

Nathaniel Believes

John 1:47–50

>   Jesus
>   said of
>   Nathaniel,
>   "Here is a man of truth and honesty.
>   Even though we have not met,
>   I know you."
>   "You know me?"
>   Nathaniel said,
>   "Rabbi, Son of God, King of Israel."
>   "I am,"
>   Jesus said.

Jesus said,
"I am
Rabbi, Son of God, King of Israel."
Nathaniel said,
"You know me?"
"I know you,
even though we have not met."
"Here is a man of truth and honesty,"
Nathaniel
said of
Jesus.

Loving Family

John 19:25–27

> Jesus did this from the cross:
> love and care for your family.
> Jesus said,
> "Mother,
> here is your
> son."

"Son,
here is your
mother."
Jesus said,
"Love and care for your family."
Jesus did this from the cross.

Baby Gifts

Matthew 2:1–12

> Magi from the east followed the star
> seeking to worship the King.
> "Where is he?"
> Herod also asked.
> The religious leaders discerned
> Bethlehem was the place
> the baby king was born.
> Herod was disturbed:
> genocide, fury, and malice.
> Responding with gifts of
> gold, frankincense, and myrrh,
> the Magi were overjoyed,
> finding Mary and the baby.

Finding Mary and the baby,
the Magi were overjoyed:
gold, frankincense, and myrrh.
Responding with gifts of
genocide, fury, and malice,
Herod was disturbed
the baby king was born.
Bethlehem was the place
the religious leaders discerned.
Herod also asked,
"Where is he?"
Seeking to worship the King,
Magi from the east followed the star.

Refugee Family

Matthew 2:13–22

> The angel said,
> Go!
> You will one day return home.
> Stay until the time
> an angel says
> Herod is dead.
> Hide the child
> and
> escape in the night.
> It is no longer necessary to
> live life in your own country.
> Things have changed.
> I will call my son
> out of Egypt.

Out of Egypt
I will call my son.
Things have changed.
Live life in your own country.
It is no longer necessary to
escape in the night
and
hide the child.
Herod is dead,
an angel says.
Stay until the time
you will one day return home.
Go!
the angel said.

Jesus' Birth

Luke 2:8–20

The angel said,
"Do not be afraid!
Hear the good news of great joy!
Savior, Messiah, Lord, is born."
As shepherds joined in
praising God,
messengers in the sky were
announcing Jesus' birth.
Messengers on the ground
began hurrying off to Bethlehem.
Everyone who heard the news
was amazed.
Mary, treasuring these moments,
continued to praise God
and
the shepherds would not be silent.

The shepherds would not be silent and
continued to praise God.
Mary, treasuring these moments,
was amazed!
Everyone who heard the news
began hurrying off to Bethlehem.
Messengers on the ground
announcing Jesus' birth.
Messengers in the sky were
praising God
as shepherds joined in:
"Savior, Messiah, Lord, is born.
Hear the good news of great joy!"
"Do not be afraid!"
the angel said.

Wedding Wine

John 2:1-11

At a Cana wedding
when faced with more guests than wine,
Mary had the solution.
There was someone who could solve this.
Despite his reluctance,
Jesus could help.
The servants saw
when the miracle happened:
six water jars became wine carafes.
Jesus turned water into wine -
the moment when
the groom's reputation was saved,
the host was astonished,
the best wine came last,
and
the last people became first
to see the first public miracle of Jesus.
Mary was beaming with pride.

Mary was beaming with pride
to see the first public miracle of Jesus.
The last people became first
and
the best wine came last.
The host was astonished,
The groom's reputation was saved
the moment when
Jesus turned water into wine.
Six water jars became wine carafes.
When the miracle happened
the servants saw
Jesus could help,
despite his reluctance.
There was someone who could solve this!
Mary had the solution
when faced with more guests than wine
at a Cana wedding.

Pilate's Questions

John 18:28–40

                                                                 "Am
I
right
you are
a king?
Most leaders don't talk to criminals
but
I am.
What
is
truth?"

"Truth
is
what
I am.
But
most leaders don't talk to criminals.
A king?
You are
right,
I
Am."

John's Identity

John 1:19–28

> "The Messiah?
> I am
> not."
> The religious leaders expect
> Elijah
> or
> the prophet.
> "So who are you?"
> "I am the voice calling in the wilderness.
> One comes after me,"
> John said.
> "who is the Messiah."
> Among you stands one
> you do not know.

You do not know
among you stands one
who is the Messiah.
John said,
"One comes after me.
I am the voice calling in the wilderness."
"So who are you?
The prophet
or
Elijah?"
The religious leaders expect
not
I am
the Messiah.

Washing Feet

John 13:1–17

> Jesus said to his disciples,
> "I want you to understand
> what I am doing.
> Washing your feet is to teach you.
> This lesson will be accomplished
> if you imitate me."
> Peter objected to having his feet washed.
> First refusing, then requesting,
> "Wash all of me!"
> You do not need to say this
> when you've already had a bath.

"When you've already had a bath
you do not need to say this:
'Wash all of me.'"
First refusing, then requesting
Peter objected to having his feet washed.
"If you imitate me,
this lesson will be accomplished.
Washing your feet is to teach you
what I am doing.
I want you to understand,"
Jesus said to his disciples.

Roof Access

Mark 2:1–12

> Four friends with faith
> help a man get to Jesus,
> who can
> heal someone
> physically and spiritually.
> Jesus wants to.

Jesus wants to
physically and spiritually
heal someone.
Who can
help a man get to Jesus?
Four friends with faith.

Calling Levi

Mark 2:13–15

> Who followed Jesus?
> There were many sinners and tax collectors,
> and they ate together,
> (after Jesus called him),
> when Levi invited Jesus to his house.

When Levi invited Jesus to his house,
(after Jesus called him),
and they ate together,
there were many sinners and tax collectors
who followed Jesus.

Jesus Tested

Matthew 4:1–11

> "Just who do you think you are?"
> I know who I am.
> My bread is God's word.
> "No!
> Throw yourself from the temple."
> As scripture is quoted out of context
> I will not fall for it.
> "I will give you the world
> if you bow down and worship me."
> You offer what is not yours;
> I worship God alone.

"I worship God alone.
You offer what is not yours."
If you bow down and worship me
I will give you the world.
"I will not fall for it,
as Scripture is quoted out of context."
Throw yourself from the temple.
"No!
My bread is God's word.
I know who I am.
Just who do you think you are?"

Stubborn Hearts

Mark 3:1–6

> On a Sabbath in the synagogue
> the Pharisees hoped for a law to be broken,
> to accuse Jesus.
> Watching for a chance
> to teach them,
> Jesus asked a simple question.
> When the people refused to answer,
> in anger and distress at their stubborn hearts,
> Jesus healed a man's hand.

Jesus healed a man's hand
in anger and distress at their stubborn hearts,
when the people refused to answer.
Jesus asked a simple question
to teach them.
Watching for a chance
to accuse Jesus,
the Pharisees hoped for a law to be broken
on a Sabbath in the synagogue.

Rejected Prophet

Mark 6:1–6

> His own people lacked faith.
> The city of
> Nazareth was amazed.
> The prophet from
> down the street
> impressed, then offended
> when they realized, "We know his family!"

When they realized, "We know his family!"
impressed, then offended.
Down the street,
the prophet from
Nazareth was amazed
the city of
his own people lacked faith.

Resurrection News

Matthew 28:1–10

The women found more than they expected
at the tomb.
How is he? "Alive!
See? He has risen!"
The lightning-earthquake-angel said,
"We entrust you to tell the others.
Come and see, then go quickly!
Jesus will be found in Galilee.
Do
not
be afraid."
Jesus said to the women,
"Hello"
and they were filled with joy!
The women were
the first to proclaim the resurrection.
The men were not.

The men were not
the first to proclaim the resurrection.
The women were,
and they were filled with joy!
"Hello!"
Jesus said to the women.
"Be afraid
not.
Do.
Jesus will be found in Galilee.
Come and see, then go quickly!
We entrust you to tell the others."
The lightning-earthquake-angel said,
"See? He has risen!"
How is he? Alive!"
At the tomb
the women found more than they expected.

Jesus' Family

Matthew 12:46–50

                                          Jesus' family gathered
                                                      outside
                                     wanting to speak to him.
                                     "My mother and brothers
                                                         are
                                                       here."
                                               Jesus said.

Jesus said,
"Here
are
my mother and brothers."
Wanting to speak to him
outside,
Jesus' family gathered.

Centurion Faith

Matthew 8:5–13

> A centurion found help in Jesus
> without Jesus going to his house.
> "We are both people with authority.
> What you say is done, even from afar.
> It takes faith
> to believe this.
> When the word is spoken
> the servant will be healed
> just as you believe."

"Just as you believe,
the servant will be healed
when the word is spoken.
To believe this
it takes faith.
What you say is done, even from afar.
We are both people with authority."
Without Jesus going to his house,
a centurion found help in Jesus.

Save Yourself

Luke 23:35–43

Rulers, soldiers, and a criminal mocked him
as
Jesus heard from the cross
their taunting insults:
focus on saving himself.
He did not
respond.
He did
when a criminal begged for mercy.

When a criminal begged for mercy
he did
respond.
He did not
focus on saving himself.
Their taunting insults
Jesus heard from the cross
as
rulers, soldiers, and a criminal mocked him.

Feeding Thousands

John 6:5–13

> "To feed the crowd
> is all we have
> five loaves and two fish?"
> Philip calculated,
> "We all know
> how many this will feed!"
> "Do we really know?
> Watch and see,"
> Jesus said.

Jesus said,
"Watch and see.
Do we really know
how many this will feed?
We all know
Philip calculated
five loaves and two fish
is all we have
to feed the crowd."

Killing Lazarus

John 12:1–11

> Who hosted a dinner for Jesus?
> Lazarus.
> Plans were also made to kill
> Jesus,
> who threatened the religious leaders.

Who threatened the religious leaders?
Jesus.
Plans were also made to kill
Lazarus,
who hosted a dinner for Jesus.

Teaching Authority

Mark 1:21–24

> The teachers of the law did not
> teach as one with authority.
> Jesus did.
> Even spirits obeyed him.
> The people were amazed.

The people were amazed
even the spirits obeyed him.
Jesus did
teach as one with authority.
The teachers of the law did not.

Last Workers

Matthew 20:1–16

> A landowner hired many that day,
> 6, 9, 12, 3, 5 o'clock.
> By hours in reverse,
> 5, 3, 12, 9, 6 o'clock,
> the last were all paid a denarius too,
> from the owner's generosity.
> The first workers complained.
> Jesus said to them,
> "The first
> will be
> the last."

"The last
will be
the first,"
Jesus said to them.
The first workers complained.
From the owner's generosity,
the last were paid a denarius too,
5, 3, 12, 9, 6 o'clock.
By hours in reverse,
6, 9, 12, 3, 5 o'clock,
a landowner hired many that day.

Index of Scriptures

Matthew
Baby Gifts—Mt. 2:1–12
Refugee Family—Mt. 2:13–22
Jesus Baptized—Mt. 3:13–17
Jesus Tested—Mt. 4:1–11
Wise Building—Mt. 7:24–27
Centurion Faith—Mt. 8:5–13
Jesus' Family—Mt. 12:46–50
Hidden Treasure—Mt. 13:44
Angels Fish—Mt. 13:47–50
Water Walking—Mt. 14:22–33
Seventy Sevens—Mt. 18:21–22
Disciples Protest—Mt. 19:13–15
Last Workers—Mt. 20:1–16
Entering Jerusalem—Mt. 21:1–11
True Obedience—Mt. 21:28–31
Resurrection News—Mt. 28:1–10

Mark
Teaching Authority—Mk. 1:21–24
Roof Access—Mk. 2:1–12
Calling Levi—Mk. 2:13–15
Stubborn Hearts—Mk. 3:1–6
Mustard Seed—Mk. 4:30–32
Suffering Woman—Mk. 5:24–34
Jairus' Daughter—Mk. 5:35–43

Rejected Prophet—Mk. 6:1–6
Bartimaeus Sees—Mk. 10:46–52
God's Image—Mk. 12:13–17
Great Offering—Mk. 12:41–44

Luke

Jesus' Birth—Lk. 2:8–20
Losing Jesus—Lk. 2:41–50
Healing Faith—Lk. 5:12–14
Good Samaritan—Lk. 10:25–37
Listening Worrying—Lk. 10:38–42
One Sheep—Lk. 15:3–7
One Coin—Lk. 15:8–10
Two Prodigals—Lk. 15:11–32
Ten Men—Lk. 17:11–19
Persistent Widow—Lk. 18:1–8
Humble Prayer—Lk. 18:9–14
Seeking Saving—Lk. 19:1–10
Save Yourself—Lk. 23:35–43

John

John's Identity—Jn. 1:19–28
Nathaniel Believes—Jn. 1:47–50
Wedding Wine—Jn. 2:1–11
Living Water—Jn. 4:1–26
Feeding Thousands—Jn. 6:5–13
Disciples Defect—Jn. 6:60–69
Killing Lazarus—Jn. 12:1–11
Washing Feet—Jn. 13:1–17
Pilate's Questions—Jn. 18:28–40
Loving Family—Jn. 19:25–27
Thomas Faith—Jn. 20:24–29